My Good Night Book

DESIGNED BY RONI AKMON

WRITTEN BY KAREN CHOPPA

COMPILED BY NANCY AKMON

ILLUSTRATIONS BY

BESSIE PEASE GUTMANN™

BESSIE PEASE GUTMANN IS A TRADEMARK OF THE BALLIOL CORP.

BLUSHING ROSE PUBLISHING
SAN ANSELMO, CALIFORNIA

For:

_____

With Love From:

_____

Date:

_____

Cover Illustration and interior illustrations by Bessie Pease Gutmann. These illustrations are reprinted with the permission of the Balliol Corporation. Designed by Roni Akmon. Text written by Karen Choppa. Compiled by Nancy Akmon

ISBN# 1-884807-51-8

Blushing Rose Publishing
P.O. Box 2238
San Anselmo, Ca. 94979
www.blushingrose.com

Printed in China

Mamma whispers, "Night, my honey", As she strokes my curly head;
She cups my chin, kisses my cheek, And tucks me into bed.
Then like bees about a flower, Angels hover near all night.
They hum lullabies and guard me, Through the darkness into light.

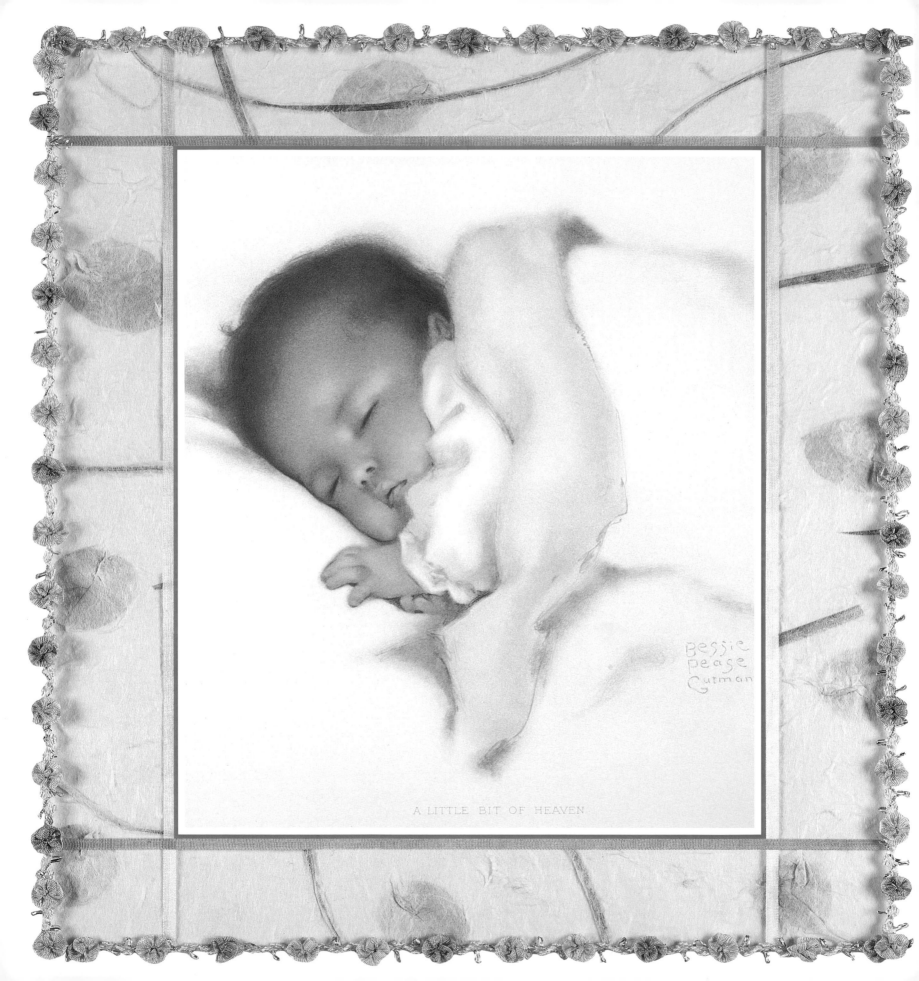

A LITTLE BIT OF HEAVEN

Bessie Pease Gutman

A LITTLE BIT OF HEAVEN

WHAT DO YOU DREAM, BABY DEAR?
WHAT FAR-OFF LULLABIES DO YOU HEAR?
BABY DREAMS OF LOVELY THINGS —
OF STARLIGHT'S GLEAM AND ANGELS' WINGS;
OF RAINBOW'S COLOR AND SUN'S BRIGHT BEAM;
WHERE THERE'S A WORLD WITHOUT SIN.
YES, A LITTLE BIT OF HEAVEN IS IN
SLEEPING BABIES AND WHAT THEY DREAM.

BABY'S FIRST CHRISTMAS

It's baby's first Christmas;
There are toys to wrap,
And the house to trim
While baby naps.
There are cards to write
While baby plays;
Baking and caroling
Fill busy days.

In the hustle and bustle
Of the holiday time,
Baby's wide-eyed wonder
Surely brings to mind

The childlike delight,
The excitement and glee
That can't be bought
And placed under the tree.

It's a renewed season
Of laughter and love,
Of accepting and giving,
Of kisses and hugs.
Just like a baby,
The world is reborn
To the joy of living
Each Christmas morn.

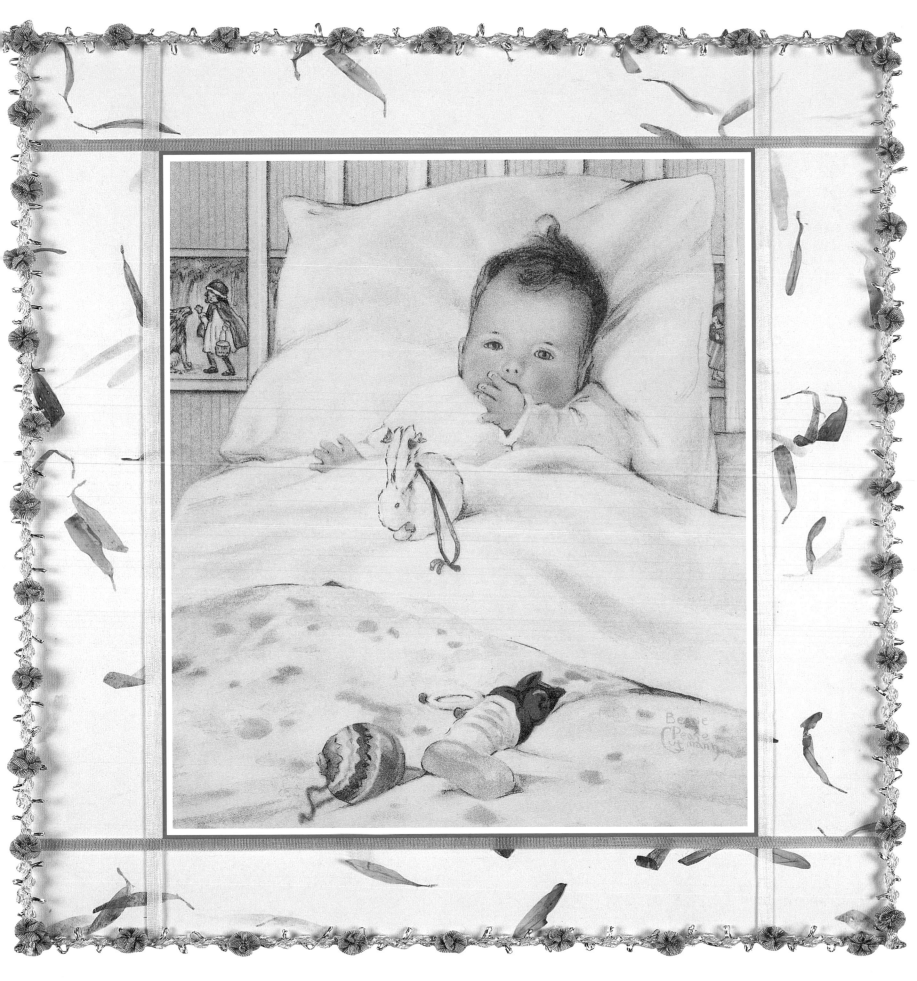

MIGHTY LIKE A ROSE

They say I'm mighty like a rose;

All soft and silky, head to toes.

My lips and cheeks are petal pink;

I'm God's most precious flower, I think.

IN PORT OF DREAMS

The rocking of the cradle
Is like the rocking of a boat;
And upon gentle waves of slumber
Baby goes afloat.

Mother's quiet humming
Becomes the winds soft sigh,
Out on the lapping waters
Beneath the starry sky.

In the harbor of the nighttime,
Baby now lies safe and snug;
In the peaceful Port of Dreams,
Wrapped in God's embracing hug.

BUTTERFLIES AND DAISIES

Never be afraid, my darling;
God will keep you in his care.
He knows the flowers of the fields
And guides winged creatures through the air.

If God watches over all these things,
From butterflies and daisies,
He must surely save a favorite spot
For someone dear as thee.

DOUBLE BLESSING

Twice the mischief,
twice the fun,
There's both a daughter
and a son.
Double bath times,
double dressings;
Two by two
go our double blessings.

A BUSY DAY

Mother always mends my clothes,
And she has taught me how to sew.
Today is a busy day for me
As I mend clothes for dolly Dee.

Mother says God is pleased
When we help those in need.
Dee will be so happy, too,
When her dress is good as new.

IN SLUMBERLAND

How like an angel you do look
In slumberland, that peaceful place.
You've put aside your wings and halo
But still you wear God's heavenly grace.

Your plump pillow for a cloud;
In place of hymn, my lullaby;
Yes, how like a sleeping angel you look
Come to earth from heaven on high.

GOOD NIGHT

"GOOD NIGHT, MOMMY.
GOOD NIGHT, DADDY.
GOOD NIGHT, TOO,
TO MY PLAYMATE, PADDY."

HE AND I
CLIMB THE STAIRS
TO OUR ROOM
AND OUR EVENING PRAYERS.

"GOD BLESS, MOMMY.
GOD BLESS, DADDY.
GOD BLESS ME AND MY
BEST FRIEND, PADDY."

TOUCHING

Did God take a
fluffy cloud
To make
my kitty's fur?
Did He put
a summer breeze
In her throat
so she would purr?

Did he put
some starlight
Into her bright
green eyes?
Am I touching
a bit of Heaven
Right here
by my side?

BUNNY

The other day I got a bunny;
The card said,
"Happy Birthday, Honey."
First I had to close my eyes;
So it would be a big surprise!

When I opened them to peek
There we were, cheek to cheek.
She is my one and only pet;
A nicer one I've never met.

She's not as frisky
as brother's pup;
She can't roll over or sit up.
She's doesn't sing like nana's bird;
She doesn't say a single word.

She's not big like cousin's pony
That I ride with sister Joanie.
She doesn't play like Auntie's cat;
She doesn't wrestle, pounce, or bat.

She is perfect, though, to me;
The very best friend a friend can be.
She's warm and cuddly,
with twitchy nose
And soft white hair
like winter snows.

I have named her Fluffy Puff,
And I can't hold her close enough.
Just like God holds me in His arms,
I, too, will keep her from all harms.

BUNNY

PALS

I am trying to be gentle
As I hug my best friend Mew
Mommy says, "Do unto others
As you'd have them do to you."
I am trying to be kind
  and loving
That is what
  get back, too,
From my purring,
  furry friend.
We're pals,
  me and kitty Mew.

SMELLING

God made me in His likeness;
He gave me ears and eyes and hair.
He gave me a nose for smelling,
The fragrance of springtime air.

A BUSY DAY IN DOLLVILLE

My family lives in Dollville; It is the nicest town.
The streets are lined with doll houses,
And there are flowers all around.
It's a busy day in Dollville
As we wash the family clothes.
Doing our chores with a happy heart
Makes work lighter as we go.

ROLLO

All creatures great and small
The Lord God made them all.
And I surely do believe
God made Rollo just for me.

SYMPATHY

Young lad Dan
Has been a naughty little man;
Tink, his pup,
Tries so hard to cheer him up.
Tink offers sympathy
As he leans on Danny's knees;
And Danny asks God
to forgive
His bad habit
to sometimes fib.

Bessie
Pease
Gutmann

ON THE UP AND UP

I watch you climb the stairs
Lifting yourself on dimpled knees;
Up and up you crawl
As patient as you please.

May you always strive to reach
The top, your goal, the peak,
No matter if it is a struggle;
May you find what it is you seek.

God, please guide his youthful step;
On the up and up let it always be.
As my little boy grows to a man
May he look forever up to Thee.

TABBY

I HAVE A CAT
HER NAME IS TABBY
WHEN I'M WITH HER
I'M ALWAYS HAPPY.
SHE'S HAPPY, TOO
BECAUSE WE PLAY
ONLY IN THE
NICEST WAY

I NEVER TUG
AT HER COAT,
OR STEP ON HER
WITH MY FOOT;
NEVER WHISKERS PULL
NOR TAIL YANK.
FOR ALL HIS CREATURES
I GIVE GOD THANKS.

LOVE'S BLOSSOM

When first I knew I carried you
You were Love's blossom that grew and grew.
God planted you within my heart
Our roots entwined, we'll never part.
To keep you strong and growing straight
I'll shower love and weed out hate.
You'll grow in grace upright and true
That wind won't sway or storm uproot.

HEARING

If I'm real, real quiet
I can hear 'most anything —
The ticking of papa's watch;
The rustling of angel wings.
It's my guardian angel I know,
'Cause I hear her whisper, too:
Katie, be still and listen;
You'll hear God say, I love you.

TAPS

You're in your sleeper
It's time for bed
You muster the soldiers
You've fiercely led.

You play taps for your troops
With tin horn to your lips
You brave leader of lead soldiers,
Of toy tanks and tiny ships.

May you remain ever steadfast
In life as in play
May you learn to always strive
To honor, trust and obey.

May you side with the truth
Battle wrongs and lies
May your voice trumpet loudly
For the honorable and wise.

SNOWFLAKES

In a world iced in white
I hop around and play
Among the fluffy snowflakes
That fell to earth today

God makes no two alike;
My Mamma told me so.
And just like a pretty snowflake,
I'm different than anyone I know.

God made us all a bit different,
With our very own faces and names;
But when He looks down upon us,
He loves us all the same.

WHO'S SLEEPY?

Who's sleepy?
Why, it's Boots and John.
Their eyelids droop;
They blink; they yawn.

Whether wake or sleeping
They are truly blest
That God who watches over them
Doesn't ever rest.

GOD IS WATCHING OVER ME,
SO I'M AS CONTENT AS I CAN BE.
HE'LL KEEP ME SAFE
FROM HURT AND HARM,
IN MY WORLD
SO GENTLE AND WARM.

Bessie Pease
Gutmann

I SIT WITH MY DOLLS ALL AROUND ME;
I GIVE THEM HUGS AND KISSES.
TOGETHER WE'RE THE HAPPY FAMILY,
MYSELF AND MY DEAR LITTLE MISSES.

I HAVE ANOTHER FAMILY;
ITS' MOMMY, DADDY, AND BROTHER.

LIKE MY DOLLS, WE LIVE HAPPILY
EACH LOOKING AFTER THE OTHER.

YET ANOTHER FAMILY LOVES ME;
AND I AM JUST ONE OF ITS DAUGHTERS.
IT IS OUR FAITHFUL FAMILY
WITH GOD AS OUR HEAVENLY FATHER.

TWO SLEEPY HEADS

Dear God, it's time to go to bed;
I rub my eyes, I nod my head.
Two sleepy heads we are I fear,
Me and cuddly dolly dear.

But before we close our eyes to sleep
We pray to you our souls to keep.
And in the morning we will say,
"Thank you, Lord, for another day."

MISCHIEF

MISCHIEF

They say I must be full of mischief;
They see the gleam in my eye.
But I've been good as good can be,
And I would never tell a lie.

Even when little sister won't tattle;
Even when mom or dad can't see;
I stay good as gold and more
So God will smile down on me.

ON DREAMLAND'S BORDERS

Under blanket blue and rose
I snuggle up to my head.
In pink and purple night clothes
Miss Sun also goes to bed.

On dreamland's border then
The day and I now rest
While Miss Moon comes out again
In her twinkling, star-strewn dress.

Elephant Dance
Memories of India

For Till, Vanessa, Nicola and Hartmut with love — T. H.

For Jake — S. M.

Barefoot Books
2067 Massachusetts Ave
Cambridge, MA 02140

This book was typeset in Veljovic
The illustrations were prepared in acrylic

Graphic design by Katie Pringle, England
Color separation by Grafiscan, Italy
Printed and bound in Hong Kong by South China Printing Co. Ltd

This book has been printed on 100% acid-free paper

Library of Congress Cataloging-in-Publication Data

Heine, Theresa.
   Elephant dance / written by Theresa Heine ; illustrated by Sheila Moxley.
      p. cm.
   Summary: Grandfather tells many stories about his native India in answer
to Ravi and Anjali's questions, such as the tale of a procession of elephants
on the feast of Divaali when he was a boy. Includes facts about life in India,
a list of cooking spices, and descriptions of Indian animals.

   ISBN 1-84148-917-4

   [1. East Indian Americans--Fiction. 2. Grandfathers--Fiction. 3. India--Fiction.]
I. Moxley, Sheila, ill. II. Title.
   PZ7.H3679El 2004
   [E]--dc22

                                                   2004004658

1 3 5 7 9 8 6 4 2

Elephant Dance

Memories of India

written by **Theresa Heine**

illustrated by **Sheila Moxley**

Barefoot Books
Celebrating Art and Story

When Grandfather came from India it was cold.
Anjali knitted him a red woollen scarf
and Ravi bought fleecy slippers for his feet.
"Is it hot in India, Grandfather?" asked Ravi.

"Yes indeed, Ravi," said Grandfather.
"The sun is a most fierce fellow,
hotter than a hundred cooking fires.
At dawn he rolls into the sky like a fiery ball,
then he uncurls and he is a ferocious tiger!

For dinner he eats red chilies.
He is so very hot and thirsty
he growls and roars all day.
In the evening, when the stars
begin to shine along the Milky Way,
he drinks a bowl of coconut milk,
and then he falls asleep."

Grandfather brought presents for everyone:

a blue sari for Mom,

a sandalwood box for Dad,

silver bangles for Anjali

and a red and gold kite for Ravi.

Grandfather and Ravi took the kite to the park.

"Grandfather," said Ravi, "what is the wind like in India?"

"When she blows from the western desert lands, Ravi,
she is strong. Like a wild horse, she stamps and snorts.
She snatches the children's kites and storms away with them,
beyond the hills and over the ocean.

"Sometimes the wind is a gentle one.
Then she pit-pats through the trees,
hushing the leaves to sleep."

"And what is the rain like?" asked Ravi, as they sheltered
under the trees.

"The monsoon rain is like a curtain, silver like Anjali's bangles.

It cascades like a waterfall from the sky,

making many mirrors on the ground.

Raindrops scurry to and fro like little silver fish.

When the sun and rain meet

they make a rainbow,

s - t - r - e - t - c - h - i - n - g

over the sky."

"Is it the same as the rainbows
I see here?" said Ravi.
"A rainbow in India, Ravi beta,
is seven silk saris hung across the sky to dry;
red as the watermelon,
orange as lentils,
yellow as saffron,
green as the parakeet,
blue as the kingfisher,

indigo as the deep ocean,

   violet as the storm-sky

      before the thunder growls."

Ravi took Grandfather shopping in the market.

They bought ghee and ginger,

fish and lentils,

FRESH   FISH

yogurt and cucumber,
and a bamboo flute for Ravi.

"Is there snow in India, Grandfather?" said Ravi.

"Yes, Ravi. High in the north are the Himalaya mountains.

The snow on their tops is a giant ice cream,

very cold and white,

melting on your tongue.

It keeps the mountain tops cool

when the tiger sun roars at midday."

It was suppertime and soon the kitchen was full of delicious smells.
Mom and Anjali cooked daal in a pan with cloves and cardamom.
They fried the fish and onion in ghee until they were golden.
Dad ground turmeric, coriander and cumin,
and mixed them with the fish and the yogurt.

Anjali fetched the rice and Ravi set the table.
Then they sat down to eat.

"Grandfather," said Ravi, "are you very old?"

"Hush now, Ravi," said Mom.

But Grandfather laughed. "Yes, Ravi beta. As you see
I am old and brown like garden soil,

and wrinkled as a walnut.

My teeth are not many and I cannot chew so well,

but I manage with what I have."

"Have you ever seen an elephant, Grandfather?" said Anjali.

"Indeed I have," said Grandfather.

"When I was a child like you and Ravi,
I saw elephants walk in a procession on the feast of Divaali.
They wore silk howdahs, blue as the royal peacock.
Princes rode on their backs.

The hot streets teemed with people,
and everywhere were flowers;
garlands of sweet jasmine and morning glory,
hibiscus blossoms, cream and red and yellow,
which we tucked behind our ears.
We ate sticky sweets of coconut and almonds
and lit fireworks in the street.
We heard the chimes of bells and gongs,
the beating of many drums."

Ravi took out his flute and blew into it.

"This is my elephant dance, Grandfather."

Grandfather smiled. "That is a most fine elephant dance.

You must practice very much and maybe one day an elephant will dance for you."

PAKISTAN

TIBET

NEPAL

THE RIVER GANGES

ARABIAN SEA

INDIA

INDIAN OCEAN

After supper Anjali got out her paints and pens, and she and Ravi
and Grandfather drew a map.

"The shape of India," said Grandfather, "is the ear of an elephant."

They drew in tigers and peacocks and crocodiles,
elephants, snakes and monkeys.

They colored in the great river Ganges
and the ice cream peaks of the
Himalayas.

They painted the western deserts,
the elephant forests of the east,
and the great tiger sun of
the south.

BHUTAN

BANGLA-
DESH

MYANMAR
(formerly BURMA)

BAY OF
BENGAL

NORTH

WEST

EAST

SOUTH

GULF OF
THAILAND

"Grandfather," said Ravi, as he got ready for bed.

"Do you love me?"

Grandfather put his arms round Ravi. "Ravi beta,

you are as warm as a newborn kid,

as soft as the frangipani blossom,

as sweet as the juice of the mango.

And I love you very much.

Now it is time for sleeping."

Ravi slept and dreamed of a deep green forest
where moonlight fell in a silver stream.
In the night grass a great gray shape swayed its head
and moved its large feet.

Ravi raised his flute to his lips
and as he played
he saw the elephant
dancing a silent dance.

Ravi's Elephant Dance

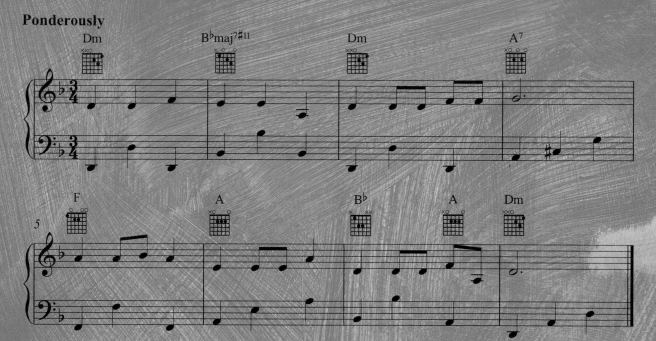

Living in India

Geography

India is in South Asia, and covers most of the Indian subcontinent. The land and sea area combined make it the sixth-largest country in the world, with a population of over a billion people.

There are three major seasons in India, and they differ from region to region. The coldest weather lasts from December to February. From March until May it is very dry and hot. The monsoon rains come in June, bringing long, heavy spells of hot, humid rain. The monsoon moves south during the summer months of June until September.

The Himalayas are a series of mountain ranges, stretching across India, Nepal, Bhutan and Tibet. The highest mountains in the world are in the Himalayas: Mount Everest, Mount K2 and Mount Kanchenjunga.

India is home to some of the largest rivers in the world, including the sacred rivers Ganges, Yamuna, and Saraswati. The river Ganges is mentioned in holy Hindu texts and holds great religious significance. Babies are frequently baptized in its waters and adults come to drink and bathe. The Saraswati river is now dry, but was considered a powerful river in ancient times.

India is one of the leading producers of wheat, cotton and rice. Wheat is a staple ingredient in North Indian cuisine, while rice is important in South and East Indian dishes. India's major cities are New Delhi, its capital city and political center, Bombay, Calcutta and Chennai.

Religion and Culture

The family in this story is Hindu. Hinduism is the main religion in India, and centers around the belief that there is one universal God, who takes the form of many different gods, both male and female. Most Hindu families revere the three gods of the Hindu trinity, or Trimurti, who are Brahma, the Creator, Vishnu, the Preserver, and Shiva, the Destroyer. Hindus worship these gods using statues, which they bathe in milk and decorate with flowers during prayer rituals. Other religions practiced in India include Sikhism, Buddhism, Islam, Christianity, Zoroastrianism and Judaism.

There are many festivals in the Hindu religion, which are calculated according to the lunar calendar, rather than the solar one. They are often celebrated with an explosion of color and joy. Elaborate meals and delicious sweets are prepared, with family and friends coming together to share in these festivities.

One of the most important Hindu festivals is Divaali, the Festival of Lights. During Divaali, Hindu families light oil lamps in their homes in honor of Lakshmi, Goddess of Wealth. They also celebrate the return of Prince Rama, hero of the Indian epic, *The Ramayana*, to his home Ayodhya after a long exile and victory over Ravana, the Demon King.

India's national flower is the lotus. This vibrant flower only grows in shallow waters, with the leaves and petals floating above the surface.

India is a country of rich cultural heritage, and the proud home of the Taj Mahal, one of the Seven Wonders of the World. This beautiful tomb was built during the Moghul empire, by its fifth Emperor Shah Jahan, in loving memory of his queen Empress Mumtaz Mahal. It took twenty-two years to complete and has become one of the most famous images in the world.

The Animals of India

Indian Elephant

The Indian elephant has been a symbol of India for centuries. It is smaller than the African elephant and is easy to tame. It is very intelligent and has an amazing sense of balance. In the hot sun, it uses its big ears as fans, flapping them to keep cool, while it sucks up water through its long trunk to use as a shower hose. Indian elephants are vegetarians and eat lots of plants and fruits, but they have a special liking for sweet treats such as mangoes, coconuts and sugar cane!

In the past, when the country was divided into many small kingdoms, Indian elephants were used to carry members of the royal families. They have also been used in forestry and to this day, they continue to help humans to protect forests from poachers. They can also be found in temple precincts and are still ridden in processions at important festivals and weddings. The "howdah" that is mentioned in this story refers to the large box-like seat, which people sit in for these processions.

Bengal Tiger

There are more wild tigers in India than in any other part of the world. They are known as Bengal or Indian tigers. There are far fewer of them now than a hundred years ago, as poachers hunt them for their fur and organs.

The orange fur and vivid black stripes of tigers make patterns that are unique

to each one, like human fingerprints. Unlike other large cats, tigers love water and are very good swimmers.

Indian Cobra

The Indian cobra is a large, poisonous snake which spits jets of venom when it is attacked. It is an important creature in Hindu culture, with the Festival of Serpents (Nagapanchami) being held in August. For this occasion, wild cobras are brought into villages to be fed, and small statues of the snake are displayed for worship.

Indian Peacock

The peacock is India's national bird, and it is thought to be sacred because it is the carrier of the Hindu god Karttikeya. It is one of the largest flying birds in the world and is most famous for its beautiful train of bright blue, golden and green feathers. Only the male peacock has this grand train, which it displays to the female to attract her.

Hanuman Langur

Hanuman langurs are a variety of monkey. They are revered across India as the descendants of the Hindu monkey god, Hanuman. Hanuman langurs are found all over India, from the mountains and forests of the Himalayas to the busy cities of the south. Many Hanuman langurs live near Hindu temples, where they are well fed by visitors. They are also accomplished thieves!

 # Food and Spices

India is famously known as "the land of spices," because of its wide array of fragrant blends and seasonings. Here are a few staples of Indian cookery:

Daal

Daal is a term used to refer to all pulses, like lentils, kidney beans and chickpeas. These pulses are used to make a stew-like dish, also called "daal," which is flavored with spices. Daal can be cooked with a variety of different pulses and is often served as an accompaniment to the main meal.

Clarified Butter (Ghee)

Ghee is a semi-liquid form of butter, in which the milk solids and water have been removed through heating and straining. It is often used as a substitute for oil in cooking and is a staple ingredient for the preparation of both sweet and savory Indian dishes.

Saffron (Kesar)

Saffron, the world's most expensive spice, comes in threads, which come from a small purple flower, the *Crocus Sativus*. It adds a bright yellow color to food and has a very strong, distinctive taste. It is used in small amounts in many sweet and savory Indian dishes, and is considered a symbol of hospitality.

Turmeric (Haldi)

This mustard yellow spice looks very similar to saffron and is often added to curries. It is thought to be lucky and is used in prayer rituals (pooja) and at weddings, when women apply it to their hands and face.

Red Chilies (Lal Mirchi)

Chilies taste as hot as they look! Red chilies add flavor and heat to popular Indian dishes like curry and daal.

Ginger (Aadrak)

Ginger is a root with a slightly peppery bite. It is a very aromatic spice which, as well as being included in savory dishes, is often added to Indian teas to help prevent colds and flu. It is also the main ingredient in snacks and drinks like gingerbread and ginger ale.

Mango (Umbri)

The mango is called the "King of Fruits" in India. This bright yellow fruit has delicious, sweet flesh which is often used in *kulfi*, an Indian ice cream flavored with saffron, almonds and milk.

Barefoot Books
Celebrating Art and Story

At Barefoot Books, we celebrate art and story with books that open the hearts and minds of children from all walks of life, inspiring them to read deeper, search further, and explore their own creative gifts. Taking our inspiration from many different cultures, we focus on themes that encourage independence of spirit, enthusiasm for learning, and acceptance of other traditions. Thoughtfully prepared by writers, artists and storytellers from all over the world, our products combine the best of the present with the best of the past to educate our children as the caretakers of tomorrow.

www.barefootbooks.com